ÅSA
GILLAND

TRACEY
TURNER

THIS IS OUR WORLD

From
ALASKA to the AMAZON
Meet 20 Children
Just Like You

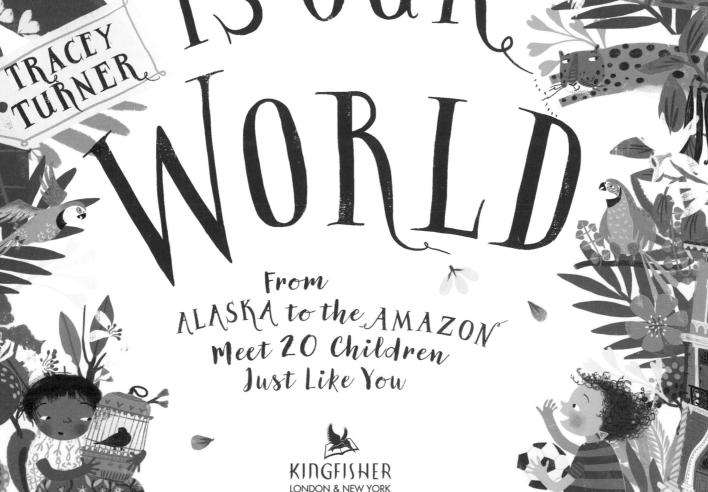

KINGFISHER
LONDON & NEW YORK

This book is for Francesca Beresford-Browne.
Great fun, huge-hearted, and utterly unforgettable,
she meant the world to us.

Thank you to . . .
. . . the Mutitjulu Community and those residents who
were involved in the editing of the text and illustration.
. . . and Leslie and Alex Norton, who told us about life
in New York City so beautifully.

A Raspberry Book
Art direction & design: Sidonie Beresford-Browne
Text: Tracey Turner
Illustration: Åsa Gilland

KINGFISHER
LONDON & NEW YORK

Distributed in the U.S. and Canada by Macmillan,
120 Broadway, New York, NY 10271

Library of Congress Cataloging-in-Publication Data has been applied for.

ISBN: 978-0-7534-7763-2

Kingfisher books are available for special promotions and premiums.
For details contact: Special Markets Department, Macmillan, 120 Broadway,
New York, NY 10271

For more information, please visit
www.kingfisherbooks.com

Printed in China
1 3 5 7 9 8 6 4 2
1TR/0322/RV/WKT/140WF

CONTENTS

INTRODUCTION

We're all human beings, but there are lots of different ways of life.
The children in this book show you some of them.

How we live often depends on where we live. We might live in a tall apartment building in a big city, and ride a bus to school. Or we might live in a village among mangrove forests, and travel to school in a boat. We might even live in the mountains, and use a zip line to whiz across a valley to get to school!

Most people in the world live in cities, like some of the children in this book, but many live in the countryside. Some people move around with their animals, as their ancestors have done for centuries. Most people's lives have changed, or are changing, to keep up with the modern world, like the Mongolian eagle hunters on page 34, or the nomadic people of the Sahara on page 26. And climate change is having an effect on all of us, especially if we live in low-lying places close to the sea, or near the warming Arctic. Some places and ways of life are more fragile than others.

Wherever and however we live, we have many more things in common than differences between us.

ALASKAN WILDERNESS, USA

SHETLAND ISLANDS, UK

NEW YORK CITY, USA

SUPAI VILLAGE, ARIZONA, USA

VENICE, ITALY

MUD-BRICK CITY OF DJENNÉ, MALI

AMAZON RAIN FOREST, BRAZIL

YUNGAS VALLEY, BOLIVIA

MAP of OUR WORLD

NORTHERN NORWAY

YAMAL PENINSULA, RUSSIA

WESTERN MONGOLIA

BEIJING, CHINA

JAPANESE COUNTRYSIDE

ROCK HOUSES OF CAPPADOCIA, TURKEY

SUNDARBANS, BANGLADESH

SAHARA DESERT

FLOATING VILLAGE, CAMBODIA

AFRICAN SAVANNA, KENYA

CENTRAL AUSTRALIA

VANUATU, SOUTH PACIFIC

SUNDARBANS

My name is Nasima and I live in the Sundarbans in Bangladesh, in a small village on an island where the jungle meets the sea. There are mangrove trees, sand dunes, and mud flats, and creeks that come and go with the tide, winding through the jungle.

I live here with my family—my brothers **Arjan** and **Debnath**, and my mom and dad. I go to school every day in a nearby town. We get there in my dad's boat.

The jungle and the sea give us everything we need—we cut firewood from the forest, collect honey from beehives, and catch fish and crabs. But there are **LOTS OF DANGERS** . . .

Ferocious tigers prowl the jungle. People used to wear a backward-facing mask to fool the tigers if they attacked from behind—but they don't work. Every year, people are killed.

There are also huge saltwater crocodiles and deadly snakes.

If someone is attacked, or gets sick, it's not easy to get to a hospital, and treatment is expensive. There's not much food or money to spare.

We pray to the goddess **Bonbibi** to protect us from danger, and promise her that we won't take more than we need from the forest.

The SUNDARBANS stretches 3,860 square miles (10,000 km²) across India and Bangladesh.

POPULATION: 2 million

LANGUAGES: Bengali, Hindi, and English

KING COBRA

BENGAL TIGER

SPOTTED DEER

SEA EAGLE

MACAQUE MONKEY

MONITOR LIZARD

Rock Houses of
CAPPADOCIA

My name is Esrin and I live in a town carved out of rock in the middle of Turkey. There's nowhere else quite like it in the whole world!

GREEK TORTOISE

The rock here is made from the ash of volcanoes that erupted millions of years ago. It formed caves, towers, and cones, and all sorts of other shapes. Hundreds of years ago, people started carving into the rock and adding stone to make buildings.

My town is called Göreme. Lots of houses are built into the rock, and some of our house is an underground cave. Inside are fire pits, where people used to cook, and alcoves in the walls that used to hold looms for weaving. The caves help keep us cool in the hot, dry summers, and warm in the cold, snowy winters.

Not all buildings in the town are built into the rock. My school is just an ordinary building.

People have lived in this area for thousands of years. Not far from here there are whole underground cities, eleven levels deep! But no one lives there now.

ROCK PILLARS KNOWN AS FAIRY CHIMNEYS

BLACK STORK

The most amazing buildings of all in Göreme are more than 30 Christian churches that were built into the rock over a thousand years ago, with beautiful artwork on the walls. Now, the churches are part of an open-air museum. Some churches have interesting names—Church of the Apple, Church of the Snake, Church of the Sandals, and Nameless Church!

BLUE ROCK LIZARD

Tourists come to see the town and the churches. Some ride in balloons to get a bird's-eye view of the landscape.

LANGUAGE: Turkish

POPULATION of GÖREME: 2,000

CAPPADOCIA is a region of Turkey of about 1,930 square miles (5,000 km²).

ALASKAN WILDERNESS

DALL SHEEP

BLACK BEAR

My name's Jack and I live in a log cabin in the middle of the Alaskan wilderness, surrounded by forest and mountains. There are no neighbors for miles. It's just me, my little sister, and my parents.

BEAVERS

MOOSE

There's no road to our cabin. To get to town we walk for two hours across streams and tundra (which is like walking on sponge in summertime), through forest and fields of tall grass. We make a lot of noise when we're walking so we don't surprise a bear. They can be really dangerous, especially if they have cubs, but if they hear you they stay away.

In the winter, it gets VERY cold. When the snow is deep enough, we use a snowmobile to get into town—it's much faster, and we can carry big, heavy things. That's how our stove and our washing machine got here.

12

CANADA GEESE

GRIZZLY BEAR

There's no running water or electricity cables to our house. We collect water from a spring, and we have solar panels. In the winter when there isn't much sunlight we have to run a generator for power as well. Dad works in San Diego but he doesn't have to go there—he works from home, in the middle of nowhere.

BALD EAGLE

We are home-schooled, so we stay here all the time. We don't have TV but we do have the internet and LOTS of books. We video-call my cousins and grandparents a lot and sometimes they come to stay. We're on our own but we don't feel lonely.

POPULATION of ALASKA: 740,000

POPULATION of USA: 327 million

LANGUAGES: English and 20 different Native American languages

VENICE

My name is Massimo and I live in a very unusual city in Italy. Instead of cars and roads there are boats and canals. Seven million tourists come here every year because Venice is the most beautiful city in the world.

Before the city was built, it was a shallow part of the lagoon. People sank deep foundations underneath the water, then built on top. Venice is actually little islands joined together by bridges, with 150 canals winding between them.

CORMORANT

The best way of getting around is on foot. My school is a 30-minute walk from my house, and you can walk right across Venice in about an hour. Or you can go by boat. The most famous boats in Venice are gondolas, which have been used for over a thousand years.

14

SEAGULL

A combination of tides and weather mean that we sometimes have "high water" that floods the streets. Either you have to wear knee-length rubber boots, or you have to know a route through the narrow streets and across bridges that avoids the flooded parts! Global warming is a big threat to Venice because it's so close to sea level.

PIGEONS

Me and my friends play soccer in the square as often as we can, but sometimes the ball bounces off into a canal and we have to fish it out with a long stick. Or a kind person in a boat throws it back!

AFRICAN SAVANNA

MAASAI POPULATION:
500,000

MAASAI LANDS are in southern Kenya and northern Tanzania, an area of about 62,000 square miles (160,000 km²).

LANGUAGES:
Maa, Swahili, English

ELEPHANT

GIRAFFES

Hello! My name is Namelok and I am a Maasai girl. I live in a village in Kenya on the Serengeti—a Maasai word that means "endless plains."

From my house you can see elephants, giraffes, zebras, lions, hyenas, and jackals. There is a big thorny fence around our houses to keep them out! There are eight houses altogether, all of them built by Maasai women. The men made the fence. My mom built our house out of sticks, mud, grass, and cattle dung.

Cattle are super important to the Maasai. The boys look after the herds of cattle and goats, and bring them into a pen at night away from predators. The cattle have bells that all make a different sound so we know which one is which without even looking.

The women and girls milk the goats and cows. On special occasions, we drink the cattle's blood—it doesn't harm the animals, and it gives us strength.

WILDEBEEST

CHEETAH

LIONS

ZEBRAS

I really like my school and my teachers. I walk there most days with my brother and two sisters. I want to be a doctor when I grow up.

After school, I help my mom collect water. In the dry season, there isn't very much of it and we have to be careful how much we use. The donkeys come with us to carry the water.

My favorite things to do are playing soccer, riding the donkeys, and listening to my mother and grandmother tell stories.

BEIJING

My name's Ning and I live in Beijing, the capital city of China. It's busy, crowded, and full of history!

POPULATION of BEIJING: 20.5 million

AREA: 6,500 square miles (16,800 km²)

LANGUAGE: Mandarin

We live in a modern apartment but old and new are mixed up together here. Not far away is the beautiful Summer Palace, built 300 years ago, full of gardens, temples, and lakes. A subway ride away is the Forbidden City, where Chinese emperors lived for 500 years. Now it's a museum open to everyone, but long ago only the emperor and his family or specially invited people could go there—intruders were executed!

Me and my mom and dad live in an apartment in the Haidan district, where there are some of the best universities in China. Lots of students live here too! My parents are both university professors. My school is close by, so I walk there.

COMMON KESTREL

BLACK STORK

There are lovely blue-sky days in Beijing, when people go to the parks to line-dance (which is VERY popular) and practice tai chi in the mornings. But we also get smog caused by exhaust fumes, power stations, and desert storms that blow dust over the city. We have to wear masks to avoid breathing in pollution.

We're also close to something even more famous than the Forbidden City—the Great Wall of China. It snakes its way across the country for more than 13,000 miles (21,000 km), with forts dotted along the way, and once kept out enemies from the North.

SIBERIAN WEASEL

AMUR HEDGEHOG

SIBERIAN CHIPMUNK

CRESTED MYNA

AMAZON

My name is Marcia and I live in the Amazon rain forest in Brazil, in a village on the banks of a great, wide river called the Tapajós.

MACAW

BLUE-CROWNED MOTMOT BIRD

I live with my parents and five brothers and sisters and our pets: a capuchin monkey named Chico and a dog named Fofo. We go to school in our village, where we learn math, reading and writing, science, history, and geography.

TAPIR

CASSAVA

My dad says we learn the most important lessons at home: how to hunt, fish, grow plants, and all about the forest and what lives in it and grows in it, what's poisonous and what isn't. The forest and the river give us all we need to live.

WHITE STORK

RAIN FOREST

AREA of MUNDURUKU
people: 9,270 square miles
(24,000 km²)

POPULATION of
MUNDURUKU: 14,000

LANGUAGES:
Munduruku, Portuguese

After school I help my mom with chores, like grinding the manioc to make flour. When that's done I love playing soccer or swimming in the river with my friends. Sometimes we see pink river dolphins.

We are Munduruku people, and once we were warriors. Now we fight threats to the forest, which are also threats to us and how we live. There are people who want to turn the forest into pasture for cows or fields of rice, and companies that want to dig up the forest or chop down all the trees. The government wants to build dams that will flood the forest and our home so as to make electricity. These things are happening all over the forest, threatening the people, animals, and plants of the Amazon.

TOUCAN

SQUIRREL MONKEY

GOLIATH BIRD-EATING SPIDER

PINK RIVER DOLPHIN

JAPANESE COUNTRYSIDE

ASIATIC BLACK BEAR

Hello, my name is Momoko and I live in a village called Kamiyama on the Japanese island of Shikoku.

I live with my mom and dad and my sister Yume. We used to live in Tokyo, which is one of the busiest, most crowded cities in the world.

In the countryside the population has fallen in the last 60 years as younger people moved to cities. There are a lot of old people here! The government encourages young people to move to the countryside. It's working: people are coming and staying because they like being far away from crowds, surrounded by beautiful mountains, countryside, and rivers.

JAPANESE PIT VIPER

At the moment my school is very small because there aren't many children here, and I will have to travel a long way when I go to high school since there isn't one in Kamiyama. But maybe soon there will be more children in school as more people come to live here, and I hope a high school will be built.

POPULATION of KAMIYAMA: 6,200

POPULATION of JAPAN: 127 million

LANGUAGE: Japanese

WILD BOAR

RED-CROWNED CRANE

My favorite time of year is the cherry blossom festival in spring, when the beautiful pink and white sakura are flowering.

CHERRY BLOSSOM

Kamiyama means "God's Mountain" in Japanese. Not far from us is an ancient Buddhist shrine. People come to Shikoku to pray at the 88 temples on the island.

23

POPULATION of
NORWAY: 5.5 million

POPULATION of
ISLAND of SØRØYA: 1,100

LANGUAGES:
Norwegian, Sami,
and English

NORTHERN NORWAY

Hello, my name is Nettie. I live in the far north of Norway, on a rocky island called Sørøya, where the tallest peaks are always covered in snow.

HUMPBACK WHALE

ORCA

My mom looks after me and my two little sisters, Ingrid and Else. She takes us to school in Hasvik, half an hour away by car.

My village is called Sørvær. Most people here earn their living from fishing, like my dad. Orcas and humpback whales often follow the fishing boats, feeding on shoals of herring and cod. There aren't as many fish as there used to be and that makes my dad worry.

ARCTIC SEAL

There's a big difference here between summer and winter. In summer, the sun never sets at all! When we're not at school we spend our time exploring tide pools, climbing rocks, and cycling around the island.

SEA EAGLE

In winter, the sun never climbs over the horizon. But even though we don't see the sun, daylight can color the skies orange, red, pink, or purple. And on clear nights, we sometimes see an amazing display—the Northern Lights flicker and flash across the sky in pink, green, yellow, purple, and blue. They're caused by electrically charged particles from space, but I like the stories that say the lights are the reflection of a great shoal of herring, or a bridge leading to the afterlife.

EIDER DUCK

ARCTIC TERN

In the dark winters me and my sisters spend a lot of time reading, and we write our own books too. Ingrid is the best at drawing and she does the pictures.

THE SAHARA DESERT

POPULATION:
2.5 million

AREA: The Tuareg live in various countries in the Sahara: Niger, Mali, Libya, Algeria, Burkina Faso, and Nigeria.

LANGUAGES:
Tamashek, French

My name is Bachir and I live in the Sahara Desert with my family. We move around the desert with our camels, cattle, and goats in search of water and grass for the animals.

We have a saying, "the desert has no secrets from the Tuareg," because our people know all there is to know about living here. We have lived in the desert for more than a thousand years, trading in gold, spices, salt, food, and clothing, never staying in one place. Our land was split up into different countries, and because of that our people have been fighting for a long time.

When I grow up I'll wear a turban with a blue veil that covers my face, like all the Tuareg men. We are sometimes called the blue men, because the cloth used to be dyed with indigo and it stained our faces blue.

Once a year there's a festival of Tuareg dance, music, and poetry. My favorite music is a Tuareg band called Tinariwen. Tinariwen means "the deserts" because to us the Sahara isn't just one desert but many.

ADDAX

FENNEC FOX

The desert is becoming drier, and many animals have died. Our traditional way of life is changing. We're going to live in a village and I'm going to go to a school with my four brothers and sisters. The school is near a well, where lots of people bring their animals to drink and graze. I think life will be easier, but my parents and especially my grandparents are sad to give up the old life.

VANUATU, SOUTH PACIFIC

My name is Monique and I live in Vanuatu in the Pacific Ocean, a chain of islands made by volcanoes and coral reefs. My island, Espiritu Santo, is covered in forest and surrounded by clear blue seas.

COCONUT CRAB

Our family are farmers—we produce coconuts, vanilla, and cocoa, and we keep pigs. In the coconut groves you sometimes see coconut crabs, which climb the trees, snap off the fruit with their pincers, then eat them where they smash on the ground!

DUGONG

During the day, the adults go to work in the gardens just outside the village and the children go to school. Me and my big sister help to look after our three younger brothers.

28

VANUATU is an archipelago of 83 tropical islands.

POPULATION of ESPIRITU SANTO: 40,000

POPULATION of VANUATU: 246,000

LANGUAGES: Bislama, English, French (but dozens of different languages and dialects are spoken)

VANUATU BANDED IGUANA

After school, we swim in the lagoons and rivers on the island or in the sea. Sometimes we see turtles and dugongs. The sea here is full of life, but it's in danger. Big aquarium companies were allowed to take fish from the reef on the island of Efate, and they have damaged the reef and taken or killed lots of fish. There are only a few beautiful hawksbill turtles left in the world, but people are fighting to save them, and there's a turtle sanctuary near Port Vila, the capital city. I want to be a marine biologist and help to save the turtles, corals, and other sea creatures.

HAWKSBILL TURTLE

There are dangers for people too. There are active volcanoes on Vanuatu, and sometimes there are earthquakes. But most dangerous are the terrible storms that can batter the islands between November and April.

SUPAI VILLAGE, ARIZONA

My name's Leo. I live in Supai, a remote village surrounded by the red walls of the world-famous Grand Canyon, in Arizona in the United States.

To get to Supai, you have to walk, ride a horse, or fly in a helicopter! We're 8 miles (13 km) from the road and everything in the town has to come that way—food, clothes, building materials, and people.

Supai is on a reservation—land controlled by Native Americans, a bit like a very small country. But we're U.S. citizens as well.

We are part of the Native American tribe Havasupai, which means People of the Blue-Green Water—close to the village is a river with turquoise-colored pools and waterfalls.

CALIFORNIA CONDOR

RED-TAILED HAWK

There are 326 reservations and 567 Native tribes in the United States.

POPULATION of SUPAI VILLAGE: 200
POPULATION of HAVASUPAI RESERVATION: 600

LANGUAGES:
Havasupai, English

Climbing down the side of the canyon to the falls is slippery and dangerous!

The Grand Canyon has been a National Park for 100 years, but Native people have lived here for thousands of years.

RATTLESNAKE

RINGTAIL CAT

MOUNTAIN LION

HOG-NOSED SKUNK

The canyon needs our protection. I wrote a letter to the President of the United States asking him to close a uranium mine near Supai, which is polluting the water for people and animals like mountain lions and California condors.

CAMBODIAN FLOATING VILLAGE

GRAY-HEADED FISH EAGLE

My name is Nou, and I live in a village called Kampong Phluk on Tonle Sap Lake in Cambodia. The village is built on stilts because for some of the year it's flooded.

SPOT-BILLED PELICAN

TONLE SAP WATER SNAKE

Tonle Sap is always a big lake, but in the rainy season it's MUCH bigger than in the dry season. You can't see the stilts at all and the houses look as though they're floating. We go everywhere by boat—to school, to the temple, to the community center, and to friends' houses.

YELLOW-HEADED TEMPLE TURTLE

In the dry season, the level of the lake water goes down by 25 feet (7.5 m)! We climb ladders up to our houses. There's a road through the village instead of water, and I get to ride my bike.

We get all our water from the lake, and most people make their living from the lake, too. I go out with my dad and help him fish, mend nets, and load the fish in ice to sell in the market. Out in the middle of the lake, you can't see the shore, just endless sparkling water.

MILKY STORK

BENGAL FLORICAN

All over Cambodia, people celebrate the Water and Moon Festival that marks the end of the rainy season. We have canoe races —the winner will have good luck for a year!

If you're small enough, anything can be a boat.

Every year, more and more tourists come to see our floating village and the mangrove forest. Some villagers drive boat taxis for them, or run floating restaurants.

WESTERN MONGOLIA

My name is Akbota and I live in Mongolia, at the foot of the Altai mountains. It's cold and windy here and not much grows, so most people are herders and hunters.

I live with my family and our goats, sheep, and camels. We live in gers, which are tent-houses that we can move as we travel. In spring, we take the animals to new pastures 60 miles (100 km) away.

LYNX

I go to school, and I would like to be a teacher one day. But my dad is an eagle hunter, one of the few people who still hunt with golden eagles, and he's going to train me to hunt with these beautiful birds. The tradition is that only boys become eagle hunters, but there's a famous girl eagle hunter named Aisholpan, and I want to be like her. You have to be an excellent rider, and very strong, because eagles are powerful enough to catch a fox.

GOLDEN EAGLE

POPULATION of MONGOLIA:
3 million

NUMBER OF EAGLE-HUNTING FAMILIES:
200

LANGUAGES:
Mongolian, Oirat, and Buryat

IBEX

Eagle hunters take an eagle from the nest when it's very young—only females because they are bigger and fiercer than males. We look after them and train them to hunt with us. They stay with us for a few years, then we release them so that they can enjoy their freedom and have chicks. It's sad to say goodbye, but it's the right thing to do.

A lot of people, like my three older brothers, move away to the city to go to university and jobs. But I hope I can stay here and hunt with eagles as well as having a job.

CORSAC FOX

35

CENTRAL AUSTRALIA

My name's Stephen and I live in the Uluru-Kata Tjuta National Park in the middle of Australia. It's a landscape of dry, grassy plains, red earth, and sacred sites.

POPULATION of MUTITJULU: 400

AREA of ULURU-KATA TJUTA NATIONAL PARK: 515 square miles (1,334 km²)

LANGUAGES: Pitjantjatjara, Yankunytjatjara, Luritja, and English

RED KANGAROO

DINGO

I live in a small community called Mutitjulu. It's only a few hundred feet from Uluru, an enormous single rock 1,175 feet (358 m) high that rises out of the desert and is special to Anangu peoples. The rock looks smooth from far away, but close up there are caves, ridges, and holes. There's also a big white scar made by the footsteps of millions of tourists who have climbed Uluru (they're not allowed to any more). If you know where to look there's art on the rock painted long ago.

My ancestors have lived here for tens of thousands of years—
ours is probably the oldest culture in the world. We have a duty
to look after the land. Grown-ups teach us Tjurkurpa—knowledge
about plants, animals, and the land, and songs, stories, and rituals
about the creation of the world.

BROWN
FALCON

There are stories about Uluru and other
sites nearby. One tells how the holes in
Uluru were made by the spears of Liru
the venomous snake man, and cracks in
the side were made by Kuniya the woma
python as she defended herself in battle.

BUDGERIGAR

THE RUFOUS
HARE WALLABY

AUSTRALIAN
RINGNECK

WOMA
PYTHON

Even though the rituals of our people are thousands
of years old, the way we live is modern. I go to school,
play video games, and swim in the town pool. But I also
learn Tjurkurpa from my family.

BLUE-TONGUED
LIZARD

THE YUNGAS VALLEY

SPECTACLED BEAR

VICUÑA

My name is Jaime and I live in the Yungas Valley in Bolivia, in the cloud forest in the foothills of the Andes mountains.

My day starts early helping Dad on the farm. He grows potatoes, corn, and oranges, and he also has a beehive. The ground and the warm, rainy climate here are good for growing crops.

LONG-TAILED MOCKINGBIRD

My school is way over on the other side of the deep valley, and I get there in an unusual way: my dad has made a zip line all the way across! The farmers use it to get around the valley. Zooming across the valley is like flying—the farmers are called "bird men," and now I'm a bird man too. When I get close to the other side, I have to pull myself along the wire. Then it's less than a ten-minute walk to school. I have friends who have to walk for two and a half hours to get to school.

38

ANDEAN CONDOR

The YUNGAS is a band of forest that lies along the Andes mountains in BOLIVIA, PERU, and ARGENTINA.

POPULATION of BOLIVIA: 11 million

LANGUAGES: Spanish, Quechua, and Aymará

SCHOOL

I love going to school and I work very hard because I want to be an engineer when I grow up. I'm going to build bridges—and my first one will be right across the valley, to replace Dad's zip line!

The school day ends at 2 pm so that everyone can get home before dark. The jungle is dangerous in the dark—in the daylight you can use a stick to check for snakes on the ground in front of you, but at night you won't see them. Plus, it's easy to slip and hurt yourself, far from help.

BUSHMASTER SNAKE

YELLOW-TAILED WOOLLY MONKEY

MUD-BRICK CITY OF DJENNÉ

My name is Komusa and I live in Djenné, capital city of Mali, which lies between the great Sahara Desert and the grasslands of the African savanna.

LITTLE EGRET

If you visit my city, one thing stands out—the Great Mosque, where me and my family and friends go to pray. It's the biggest mud building in the whole world, built from bricks that are made of mud, sand, rice husks, and water, and dried in the sun. Inside there are 99 pillars that stand for the 99 names of God.

EGYPTIAN PLOVER

GREAT MOSQUE

BLACK-SHOULDERED KITE

Everyone joins in the Plastering of the Great Mosque festival every year. The women bring the water and the men mix the mud plaster ready for the masons—my dad is one of them! Musicians play while everyone works and there's lots of food. We always have fun but it's also necessary—the Mosque would fall down if we didn't look after it.

I live with my mom, dad, brother, Amadou, and sister, Asetou. Our house is built from mud just like the Great Mosque. My dad replasters it before the rainy season, along with lots of other houses. I'm learning to be a mason just like him. I have to fetch and carry, and later I'll learn the secret magic words that only Djenné masons know.

Mud-brick houses are cooler in summer and warm in winter, but some people wish they could live in a concrete house because then they wouldn't have to replaster every year. I don't, though!

MALI is a landlocked country in AFRICA.

POPULATION of DJENNÉ: 33,000

LANGUAGES:
French, Bambara, Fulfulde, Tamashek, Dogon, and Songhai

NEW YORK CITY

HERRING GULL

RED FOX

HOUSE SPARROW

Hi, I'm Alex. I live in New York City near 125th Street, in a neighborhood called Harlem.

I live with my mom in a big complex of six apartment buildings. There's a games room and a playground, and a Japanese restaurant where we go for special occasions. The trees are full of birds, and on summer evenings twinkling lightning bugs light up the branches.

NEW YORK CITY is the most densely populated city in the UNITED STATES.

POPULATION of NEW YORK CITY: 8.5 million

LANGUAGES:
English, Spanish, and lots of other languages are spoken in the city.

We live high up on the 19th floor, which is great because I can see barges and tugboats on the river, planes flying in and out of the airport, and helicopters coming to land in the city. The subway breaks above ground near our building and we watch it far below, like a toy train set. It's not so great up here when the elevator doesn't work, though.

My school is about one and a half miles away. I get there by bus or taxi with my neighbors, Ravi and Jatin.

Our complex is near Riverside Park and not far from Central Park, where I love playing soccer and riding my bike. I also like fishing in the lake in Central Park and in the Hudson River. Once I went on a fishing boat in the harbor, and we caught two big flounder. We made sushi!

GRAY SQUIRREL

WHITE-TAILED EAGLE

SHETLAND PONIES

My name's Connor, and I live on a windswept island far out in the North Sea between mainland Scotland and Norway.

COMMON SEAL

OTTER

I live on the biggest of the Shetland Islands, which is called Mainland. There are hundreds of islands here but people only live on sixteen of them. There are bridges connecting some of them, and ferries run between others. The islands' names—Unst, Yell, Fetlar, Mousa, Muckle Flugga—come from the old Norse language, because Vikings lived here long ago.

My school is in Lerwick, the capital of Mainland. We're taught the same as at schools in mainland Scotland, which is over 100 miles (160 km) away over the sea. My brother Jamie goes to the local secondary school where Mom's a math teacher.

ISLANDS

In the summer it barely gets dark at night this far north. We go for picnics on the beach, and swim in the cold, clear sea. We sometimes see orcas hunting seals.

HUMPBACK WHALE

ORCA

PUFFIN

In midwinter the days are very short —the sun doesn't come up until after nine in the morning, and it sets before 3 pm. But something special happens during the dark days of January—a festival called Up Helly Aa. We spend all year making a beautiful Viking boat, and then . . . we set fire to it! There's a long procession where everyone dresses up, and lots of fun and feasting. One Shetland man is elected to be the Jarl, who's in charge of the festival. The other 900 people who take part are called Guizers.

POPULATION of SHETLAND ISLANDS: 23,000

POPULATION of SCOTLAND: 5.4 million

LANGUAGES: Shetland Scots, Scots Gaelic, and English

YAMAL PENINSULA

NENETS POPULATION:
45,000

AREA of YAMAL
PENINSULA: 47,000
square miles (122,000 km²)

LANGUAGES:
Nenets (two dialects, Forest
and Tundra) and Russian

TUNDRA WOLVES

TUFTED DUCK

My name is Nyadma and I live in
the far north of Russia on the Yamal Peninsula,
which means "edge of the world" in my language.
I belong to the Nenets people. We move about
the tundra and forest with our herds of reindeer.

Reindeer are VERY important to us. They are our
transport, food, shelter, and clothes. We eat their meat,
make clothes and tents from skins, make thread from
tendons, and parts for sleds from bones. Clothes made
of reindeer skin give us special protection.

ARCTIC FOX

Our house is called a mya, a tent made
of reindeer hides (and sometimes other
fabric) attached to long wooden poles.
It's easy to pack up and carry as we
move about with the herd.

In the winter, the children don't stay with the rest of the clan. From autumn to spring we stay in a boarding school in the town of Vorkuta, where we learn the same as other Russian children. The temperature can drop to -58°F (-50°C) and the grown-up Nenets go south to the forests, where the reindeer graze on lichen and moss. In summer we go back to our families and travel north, when there's food for the reindeer on the tundra. We miss our families when we're at school.

SNOW BUNTING

MUSK OX

The land is changing. Ice melts earlier than it used to and freezes later, and the permanent ice is starting to melt. Underneath our frozen lands there is oil and gas. Companies are drilling the pastures. Explosions and leaks have destroyed the land. We pray that we can continue our traditional way of life.

REINDEER

RINGED PLOVER

47

INDEX